Choc

igloo

Published by Igloo Books Ltd
Cottage Farm
Sywell
NN6 0BJ
www.igloo-books.com

10 9 8 7 6 5 4 3 2 1

ISBN: 978 1 84852 731 7

Project Managed by R&R Publications Marketing Pty Ltd

Food Photography: R&R Photostudio (www.rrphotostudio.com.au)
Recipe Development: R&R Test Kitchen

Front cover photograph © Stockfood/David Loftus
Printed in and manufactured in China

Contents

Banana Choc Chip Soufflés

Preparation 30 mins **Cooking** 15 mins **Calories** 146

3 large egg whites

⅓ cup sugar

2 firm, ripe bananas, about 170g (6oz) each

2½ tbsps bittersweet chocolate chips

1 Preheat oven to 220°C (425°F) and lightly butter six ¾-cup ramekins.

2 Beat egg whites until they just hold soft peaks, then gradually beat in sugar until meringue holds stiff peaks. Coarsely grate bananas onto meringue and gently fold chocolate chips into meringue.

3 Arrange ramekins on a baking sheet and divide mixture evenly among them. Run a knife around sides of ramekins, freeing mixture to aid rising, and bake soufflés in middle of oven until puffed and golden brown, about 15 minutes. Serve immediately.

Serves 6

Black and White Tart

Preparation 2 hrs 35 mins **Cooking** 30 mins **Calories** 713

2 egg whites
½ cup superfine sugar
220g (7oz) shredded coconut
¼ cup plain flour, sifted

Chocolate Sour Cream Filling
2 egg yolks
¾ cup heavy cream
185g (6oz) bittersweet chocolate
2 tbsps cognac or brandy
185g (6oz) white chocolate
⅔ cup sour cream

Raspberry Coulis
250g (9oz) raspberries
1 tbsp confectioner's sugar, sifted

Variation: You could use 250g (9oz) of strawberries instead of raspberries .

1 Preheat oven to 180°C (350°F). Place egg whites in a bowl and beat until soft peaks form. Gradually beat in superfine sugar. Fold in coconut and flour. Press mixture over base and up sides of a buttered and lined 23cm (9in) springform flan tin. Bake for 20–25 minutes or until golden. Stand in tin for 5 minutes then remove and place on a wire rack to cool.

2 To make filling, place egg yolks and cream in a heatproof bowl set over a saucepan of simmering water and beat until thick and pale. Stir in bittersweet chocolate and cognac or brandy and continue stirring until chocolate melts. Remove bowl from pan and set aside to cool.

3 Place white chocolate and sour cream in a heatproof bowl set over a saucepan of simmering water and heat, stirring, until smooth. Remove bowl from pan and set aside to cool. Place alternating spoonfuls of dark and white mixtures in macaroon shell and, using a skewer, swirl to give a marbled effect. Chill for 2 hours or until filling is firm.

4 To make coulis, place raspberries in a blender and process to make a purée. Press purée through a sieve to remove seeds, then stir in confectioner's sugar. Serve with tart.

Serves 8

Chocolate Cookie Pudding

Preparation 15 mins **Cooking** 55 mins **Calories** 477

8 x 4 day-old chocolate cookie, crumbled

½ cup sugar

⅓ cup cocoa powder

¼ tsp ground cinnamon

¼ tsp salt

2 eggs

2 cups milk

½ tsp vanilla extract

1 tbsp vegetable oil

1 Preheat oven to 180°C (350°F). Lightly butter a 20 x 20cm (8in) baking dish. Cover the bottom of the baking dish with an even layer of the crumbled cookies.

2 In a small bowl, mix the sugar, cocoa, cinnamon and salt.

3 In a medium bowl, beat together the eggs, milk, vanilla and vegetable oil. Add the sugar mixture and stir until combined.

4 Pour evenly over the cookies. Press down with the back of a large spoon.

5 Place the baking dish into a larger, high-sided baking dish. Pour boiling water halfway up the sides of the outside dish. Bake for 55 minutes, or until set.

Serves 4

Banana Split

Preparation 10 mins **Calories** 836

½ cup whipping cream

4 small ripe bananas

3 cups vanilla ice cream

⅔ cup ready-made chocolate sauce

½ cup walnuts or mixed nuts, chopped

1 Beat the cream in a bowl until it has thickened and holds its shape when lifted with a spoon.

2 Peel the bananas, slice in half lenthways and lay in four shallow dishes or bowls. Drag a tablespoon along the top of the ice cream to form a ball. Place two balls of ice cream between each banana half.

3 Decorate each banana split with a quarter of the whipped cream, chocolate sauce and chopped walnuts. Serve straight away.

Variations: Serve scoops of your favorite ice cream in ready-made brandy snap baskets. Or chop some stem ginger in syrup and sprinkle over bowls of ice cream, with a little of the syrup. Liqueurs are also wonderful with ice cream: Grand Marnier goes well with strawberry, Bailey's Original Irish Cream complements chocolate and almost anything tastes good with vanilla.

Serves 4

Chocolate Macadamia Pudding

Preparation 25 mins **Cooking** 2 hrs **Calories** 510

175g (6oz) self-rising flour
2 heaped tbsps cocoa powder
125g (4½oz) butter, softened
125g (4½oz) superfine stet
2 large eggs
65g (2½oz) bittersweet chocolate (55 to 65% cocoa solids), chopped
75g (2¾oz) unsalted macadamia nuts, toasted and chopped into large chunks
3 tbsps milk

1 Sift and mix the flour and cocoa together. In a separate bowl combine the butter and sugar and cream them together until pale and fluffy.

2 Beat in the eggs one at a time, adding a little of the flour mixture with the second egg. Fold in the remaining flour mixture and gently combine. Add the chocolate, nuts and milk.

3 Spoon the mixture into a greased 1-litre (2 pint) bowl or separate bowls. Cover bowls with a layer of greased aluminum foil in a domed shape to allow for the mixture to rise.

4 Secure the foil with string. Place bowls in a simmering pot of water or steamer that has enough water to cover halfway up the sides of the dish.

5 Steam for ½ to 2 hours, topping up with hot water if necessary. Serve with a swirl of cream on top.

Serves 6

Chocolate Pear Delights

Preparation 10 mins **Cooking** 15 mins **Calories** 699

3 sheets puff pastry, thawed

1 cup milk chocolate buttons, melted

825g (1¾lb) canned pear halves, drained and sliced 5mm (⅕in) thick

⅓ cup almond meal

Alternative: You can use apricots instead of pears.

1 Preheat oven to 200°C (400°F) and line 2 oven trays with baking paper. Using a 14cm (5in) plate as a stencil, cut out 2 rounds from each pastry sheet, making a total of 6 rounds. Pierce each pastry round all over with a fork, leaving a 1cm (⅓in) border, then place on the prepared oven trays.

2 Spread each round with 1–2 tbsps of melted chocolate, leaving a 1cm (⅓in) border. Add the sliced pear halves and almond meal to a bowl and gently mix to combine. Divide the pear slices evenly between the pastry rounds and arrange decoratively. Bake for 12–15 minutes. Serve with ice cream, and if you prefer, drizzle with melted chocolate.

Note: One of the easiest ways to melt chocolate is to place chopped chocolate in a microwave-safe container and cook on high in 30-second bursts, stirring a little each time until melted.

Serves 6

Chocolate Pudding

Preparation 1 hr **Cooking** 5 mins **Calories** 500

⅓ cup cocoa powder
¼ cup cornstarch
1 cup superfine sugar
2 cups skimmed milk or soymilk
15g (½oz) margarine
1 cup fresh fruit, for example, blueberries, chopped strawberries or raspberries

1 Put all dry ingredients into a saucepan with the cold milk. Stir and place on the stove. Bring to a boil, stirring constantly, then simmer for 2 minutes.

2 Add margarine and stir. Pour into serving bowl. To prevent a skin from forming on the pudding, place a sheet of baking paper directly on the pudding surface while still warm.Cool, decorate with fresh fruit and serve.

Serves 4

Cookies and Cream Semi-Freddo

Preparation 10 mins plus 6 hrs chilling **Calories** 950

3 egg yolks

1 can condensed milk

4 tsps vanilla extract

1 cup chocolate cookies, crushed

2 cups whipping cream

1 In a large bowl, beat the egg yolks, then stir in the condensed milk and vanilla. Fold in the cookies and cream.

2 Pour mixture into a 23 x 12cm (9 x 4½in) loaf tin lined with aluminum foil. Cover and freeze for 6 hours or until firm. To serve, scoop from tin or cut into slices.

Serves 4

Frosted Fruit with White Chocolate Cream

Preparation 5 mins plus 1 hr freezing **Cooking** 5 mins **Calories** 322

750g (1¾oz)mixed fresh or frozen red fruit, such as cherries, raspberries and strawberries, hulled if fresh

2 x 150g (5oz) bars luxury white chocolate, broken into pieces

5 tbsps low-fat natural yogurt

1 If using fresh fruit, place it in a shallow freezer container and put into the freezer for 1 hour. If using frozen fruit, keep it frozen.

2 Divide the fruit between small serving bowls. Put the chocolate and yogurt into a small saucepan and cook over a low heat for 5 minutes or until the chocolate has melted, stirring occasionally and taking care not to let it boil. Spoon or pour the mixture over the frosted fruit and serve.

Serves 6

Frozen Maple and Nut Parfait

Preparation 5 hrs 40 mins Calories 653

6 egg yolks
1 cup superfine sugar
½ cup maple syrup
2½ cups heavy cream
100g (4oz) macadamias, finely chopped
100g (4oz) white chocolate, chopped

1 Place egg yolks in a bowl and beat until thick and pale. Place sugar and ½ cup water in a saucepan and heat over a low heat, stirring, until sugar dissolves. Bring to the boil and boil until mixture thickens and reaches soft ball stage or 118°C (245°F) on a sugar thermometer.

2 Gradually beat sugar mixture and maple syrup into egg yolks and continue whisking until mixture cools. Place cream in a bowl and beat until soft peaks form. Fold cream, macadamias and chocolate into egg mixture.

3 Pour mixture into an aluminum foil-lined 15 x 25cm (5½ x 10in) loaf tin and freeze for 5 hours or until firm.

4 Turn parfait onto a serving plate, remove foil, cut into slices and drizzle with extra maple syrup.

Note: Can be served with fresh fruit and perhaps some almond-flavored biscotti.

Serves 8

Hot Brownies with White Chocolate Sauce

Preparation 20 mins   **Cooking** 40 mins   **Calories** 576

100g (4oz) soft margarine, plus extra for greasing

100g (4oz) soft dark brown sugar

1 large egg, beaten

1 tbsp corn syrup

1 tbsp cocoa powder, sifted

50g (2oz) wholewheat self-rising flour, sifted

25g (1oz) pecan nuts or walnuts, chopped

Sauce

1 tbsp cornstarch

200ml (7 fl oz) whole milk

50g (2oz) white chocolate, broken into small chunks

1 Preheat the oven to 180°C (350°F). Grease the sides and base of an 18cm (7in) square cake tin. Beat the margarine and sugar in a bowl until pale and creamy, then beat in the egg, syrup, cocoa powder and flour until it forms a thick, smooth batter. Stir in the nuts.

2 Spoon the mixture into the tin, smooth the top and bake for 35–40 minutes, until well risen and just firm to the touch.

3 Meanwhile, make the sauce. Blend the cornstarch with 1 tbsp of the milk. Heat the rest of the milk in a saucepan, add the cornstarch mixture, then gently bring to the boil, stirring as the sauce thickens. Cook gently for 1–2 minutes.

4 Add the white chocolate, then remove from the heat and stir until it melts. Cut the brownies into 8 pieces and serve warm with the chocolate sauce.

Serves 4

Ice Cream with Hot Chocolate Sauce

Preparation 5 mins   **Cooking** 15 mins   **Calories** 376

30g (1oz) cocoa powder, sifted

300ml (11oz) boiling water

50g (2oz) soft light or dark brown sugar

30g (1oz) butter

1 tbsp corn syrup

4 servings vanilla ice cream

1 Place the cocoa powder and the boiling water in a small saucepan, stir to combine, then gently bring to the boil. Reduce the heat and simmer for 10 minutes or until reduced by about three-quarters, beating from time to time.

2 Stir in the sugar, butter and corn syrup and cook gently for 2–3 minutes, until the sugar and butter have melted and the sauce looks shiny.

3 Put the ice cream into 4 bowls. Pour over the hot chocolate sauce and serve straight away.

Note: This chocolate sauce is made with cocoa powder, but it has such a rich, scrumptious flavor that you'd think it was made from the best-quality chocolate and nothing else!

Serves 4

Macaroon-Stuffed Pears with Chocolate

Preparation 30 mins **Cooking** 40 mins **Calories** 571

8 large pears
100g (4oz) butter
200g (7oz) superfine sugar
100ml (4 fl oz) red wine
250g (9oz) coconut macaroons
1 egg
½ cup bread crumbs
½ cup grated chocolate
1 cup milk
2 tbsps sugar, extra
2 tbsps light brown sugar

1 Peel then cut the pears in half and remove pips and core with a sharp knife, leaving a cavity large enough for the filling.

2 Melt the butter and add the sugar, add the wine and stir gently until the sugar dissolves. Add the pear halves, cut side down in the syrup and cook on a low heat for about 10 minutes. Turn the pears once toward the end of the cooking time.

3 Remove the pears from the syrup and then boil the syrup to reduce. Take care not to allow the syrup to burn. Spoon one dessert spoon of syrup over each pear.

4 Crush the macaroons and set aside. Mix the bread crumbs and chocolate with the milk and 2 tbsps sugar and set aside for 10 minutes. When the milk has been absorbed, add the crushed macaroons and egg. Mix well.

5 Spoon this filling into the pear cavities and sprinkle with light brown sugar. Bake at 200°C (400°F) for 10 minutes, then broil briefly (if desired) to melt sugar. Serve with cream or vanilla ice cream.

Serves 8

Mandarin and Chocolate Layers

Preparation 15 mins plus 5 mins cooling **Cooking** 5 mins **Calories** 600

100g (4oz) bittersweet chocolate, broken into pieces

200ml (7 fl oz) crème fraîche

4 tbsps natural yogurt

zest of 1 orange

zest of 1 lemon

150g (5oz) Graham Crackers

620g (1¼lb) canned mandarin segments, drained

Variation: You can use orange segments instead of mandarins.

1 Melt the chocolate in a bowl placed over a pan of simmering water, then leave to cool for 5 minutes. Add the crème fraîche, yogurt and orange zest to the chocolate (reserving a few strips of zest for decoration) and mix together well.

2 Put the crackers into a plastic bag and roughly crush with a rolling pin. Divide half the crushed crackers between 4 dessert glasses, then top with a layer of the chocolate mixture.

3 Spoon in the mandarins, reserving a few segments for decoration, then sprinkle the remaining crushed crackers over them. Top with the remaining chocolate mixture and the reserved mandarins and decorate with the zest.

Serves 4

Chocolate-Mocha Cake

Preparation 30 mins **Cooking** 30 mins plus 2 hrs chilling time **Calories** 634

185g (6oz) bittersweet chocolate, broken into small pieces

4 eggs, separated

½ cup superfine sugar

185g (6oz) sweetened butter, softened and cut into pieces

2 tbsps strong black coffee

½ cup plain flour

Chocolate glaze

200g (7oz) bittersweet chocolate, broken into small pieces

100g (4oz) sweetened butter

2 tbsps water

1 Place chocolate in top of a double saucepan and heat over simmering water for 5 minutes, or until chocolate melts. Remove top pan from heat and stir until smooth. Set aside to cool.

2 Preheat oven to 160°C (325°F). Place egg yolks and sugar in a bowl and beat until pale and fluffy. Add butter and beat mixture until creamy. Add coffee and chocolate and continue whisking mixture until creamy. Sift flour over mixture and fold in lightly.

3 Beat egg whites until soft peaks form. Lightly fold egg-white mixture into chocolate mixture. Pour into a greased and lined 20cm (8in) round cake tin and bake for 30 minutes or until firm to touch. Turn off oven and cool cake in oven with door ajar. Remove from tin and refrigerate for 2 hours or overnight.

4 To make glaze, place chocolate, butter and water in top of a double saucepan and heat over simmering water until chocolate and butter melt. Remove top pan from heat and stir ingredients to combine. Set aside to cool.

5 Remove cake from refrigerator and place on a wire rack. Place on a tray and pour glaze over cake, smoothing it over edges and onto sides with a spatula. Leave until completely set. Transfer cake to a flat serving platter and cut into slices to serve.

Serves 8

Blissful Chocolate Bombe

Preparation 24 mins plus 2 hrs freezing **Calories** 570

Vanilla ice cream

220g (7oz) superfine sugar

8 egg yolks

660ml (22 fl oz) cream

1 vanilla bean

375ml (13 fl oz) whipping cream

Chocolate mousse

175g (6oz) bittersweet chocolate, chopped

3 tbsps strong black coffee

4 eggs, separated

15g (½ oz) butter, softened

1 tbsp brandy

3 tbsps superfine sugar

125ml (4 fl oz) whipping cream

1 To make ice cream, place sugar and egg yolks in a bowl and beat until thick and creamy. Place cream and vanilla bean in a heavy-based saucepan and simmer for 3 minutes. Cool slightly, then remove vanilla bean.

2 Gradually add 250ml (8 fl oz) of the warmed cream to egg mixture, whisking well. Add egg and cream mixture to remaining cream, stirring over low heat until mixture coats the back of a spoon. Set aside to cool.

3 Stir cream mixture, pour into a freezerproof tray lined with plastic food wrap, and freeze until almost set. Break up mixture with a fork and place in blender. Process until mixture is thick and creamy. Pour ice cream into a chilled mould (9-cup capacity) lined with plastic food wrap. Push a smaller mould, covered with plastic food wrap, into centre of ice cream, forcing ice cream up around the sides of the mould. Freeze until firm.

4 To make chocolate mousse, place chocolate in a bowl and melt over hot water, stirring until smooth. Add coffee. Remove from heat and beat in egg yolks one at a time. Continue whisking and add butter and brandy. Allow mixture to cool.

5 Beat egg whites until soft peaks form, then beat in sugar. Fold egg whites and cream through chocolate mixture. Remove smaller mould from ice cream. Spoon mousse into centre of ice cream and return to freezer until set.

Serves 12

Caramel Walnut Petits Fours

Preparation 35 mins **Cooking** 10 mins **Calories** 184 (each)

1 cup sugar
½ cup brown sugar
2 cups heavy cream
1 cup corn syrup
60g (2oz) butter, chopped
½ tsp baking soda
150g (5oz) walnuts, chopped
1 tbsp vanilla extract
Chocolate frosting
375g (13oz) bittersweet or milk chocolate, melted
2 tsps vegetable oil

Variation: You can use toasted almonds instead of walnut.

1 Place sugar, brown sugar, cream, corn syrup and butter in a saucepan and heat over a low heat, stirring constantly, until sugar dissolves. As sugar crystals form on sides of pan, brush with a wet pastry brush.

2 Bring syrup to the boil and stir in baking soda. Reduce heat and simmer until syrup reaches the hard ball stage or 120°C (248°F) on a sugar thermometer.

3 Stir in walnuts and vanilla and pour mixture into a buttered and foil-lined 20cm (8in) square cake tin. Set aside at room temperature for 5 hours or until caramel sets.

4 Remove caramel from tin and cut into 2cm (¾in) squares.

5 To make frosting, combine chocolate and oil. Half-dip caramels in melted chocolate, place on baking paper and leave to set.

Note: For easy removal of the caramel from the tin, allow the foil lining to overhang the tin on two opposite sides to form handles.

Makes 40

Chewy-Gooey Chocolate Marshmallow Slice

Preparation 20 mins **Cooking** 12 mins **Calories** 325 (each)

250g (9oz) chocolate whole wheat cookies
100g (4oz) butter
¼ cup sugar
3 tbsps cocoa
1 egg
1 tsp vanilla extract
2 cups white marshmallows
½ cup coconut

1 Crush cookies in a plastic bag or chop in a blender until medium-coarse crumbs. Melt butter with sugar and cocoa in a saucepan large enough to mix all the ingredients.

2 Remove from heat. Cool slightly, then beat in egg and vanilla extract until combined. Press into an 28 x 18cm (11 x 6¼in) tin with a baking paper-lined base.

3 Melt marshmallows over a low heat. Mix in coconut. Spread over chocolate base. Refrigerate until set. Cut into small squares or fingers. Store in freezer and eat while frozen.

Makes 12

Chocky Road Cookies

Preparation 20 mins **Cooking** 10 mins **Calories** 253 (each)

180g (6oz) butter, at room temperature

1 cup brown sugar

2 eggs, lightly beaten

2½ cups plain flour

½ cup cocoa powder

½ cup buttermilk

185g (6oz) white chocolate, roughly chopped

1 cup dry-roasted peanuts

1 cup chocolate chips

1 Preheat oven to 180°C (350°F). Lightly butter 2 baking trays.

2 Place the butter and sugar in a bowl and beat until light and fluffy. Gradually beat in the eggs.

3 Sift together the flour and cocoa powder. Add the flour mixture, buttermilk, white chocolate, peanuts and chocolate chips to the egg mixture and combine well.

4 Drop tablespoonfuls onto the baking trays and bake for 10 minutes or until cooked. Transfer to wire racks to cool.

Makes 36

Chocolate Panforte

Preparation 25 mins **Cooking** 25 mins **Calories** 243 (each)

1 cup liquid honey

1 cup sugar

250g (9oz) almonds, toasted and chopped

250g (9oz) hazelnuts, toasted and chopped

125g (4½oz) candied apricots, chopped

125g (4½oz) candied peaches, chopped

100g (4oz) candied mixed peel

1¼ cups plain flour, sifted

¼ cup cocoa powder, sifted

2 tsps ground cinnamon

155g (5½oz) bittersweet chocolate, melted

rice paper

1 Preheat oven to 200°C (400°F). Place honey and sugar in a small saucepan and heat, stirring constantly, over a low heat until sugar dissolves. Bring to the boil, then reduce heat and simmer, stirring constantly, for 5 minutes or until mixture thickens.

2 Place almonds, hazelnuts, apricots, peaches, mixed peel, flour, cocoa powder and cinnamon in a bowl and mix to combine. Stir in honey syrup. Add chocolate and mix well to combine.

3 Line an 18 x 28cm (6¾ x 11in) shallow cake tin with rice paper. Pour mixture into tin and bake for 20 minutes. Turn onto a wire rack to cool, then cut into small pieces.

Makes 32

Chocolate Peanut Cookies

Preparation 20 mins **Cooking** 15 mins **Calories** 242 (each)

¾ cup plain flour
¼ teaspoon baking soda
½ teaspoon salt
125g (4½oz) sweetened butter, at room temperature
¾ cup brown sugar
2 tbsps superfine sugar
1 vanilla pod, split in half lenthways
1 egg
3 teaspoons milk
1 cup rolled oats
1 cup unsalted peanuts
1 heaped cup bittersweet chocolate chips

1 Preheat oven to 160°C (325°F). Line 2 baking trays with baking paper.

2 Combine flour, baking soda and salt in a bowl.

3 Beat the butter, brown sugar, superfine sugar and seeds from vanilla pod in a blender until the mixture has become thick and pale.

4 Add the egg and milk, then beat in the flour mixture with the rolled oats. Fold in the peanuts and chocolate.

5 Drop tablespoonfuls of the dough onto the baking trays. Bake for 15 minutes, then remove from the oven and allow to cool on a wire rack.

Makes 25

Chocomarsh Cookies

Preparation 30 mins **Cooking** 12 mins **Calories** 275 (each)

60g (2oz) butter, at room temperature

½ cup brown sugar, firmly packed

1 egg

2 tsps vanilla extract

1½ cups plain flour, sifted

½ cup superfine sugar

¾ tbsps gelatine powder

150g (5oz) bittersweet chocolate, melted

¼ cup confectioner's sugar

1 Preheat oven to 160°C (325°F). Line a baking tray with baking paper.

2 Cream butter and brown sugar in a large bowl until smooth. Add egg and 1 teaspoon of vanilla and mix well. Fold in flour.

3 Place mixture on a lightly floured surface and roll out to 5mm (⅕ in) thickness. Cut out circles with a 6cm (2⅓ in) round cookie cutter and place on the baking tray.

4 Bake for 10–12 minutes or until golden and cooked. Cool on trays.

5 Meanwhile, combine superfine sugar and ½ cup water in a small saucepan, then sprinkle in gelatine powder. Stir over low heat until sugar and gelatine dissolve. Bring to the boil, then reduce heat and simmer for 4 minutes. Remove and cool.

6 When almost cold, pour mixture into a bowl, add remaining vanilla and process in a blender for 3–4 minutes until very thick.

7 Spoon marshmallow mixture into a pastry bag fitted with a plain 1cm (⅓ in) tip and pipe onto half the cookies. Top with remaining cookies, pressing gently. Place cookies in refrigerator for about 15 minutes until marshmallow is firm.

8 Remove from refridgerator, spread with melted chocolate and dust with confectioner's sugar.

Makes 12

Crunchy Choc Cookies

Preparation 10 mins **Cooking** 10 mins **Calories** 254 (each)

1 cup crunchy peanut butter

200g (7oz) butter, at room temperature

1 tbsp vanilla extract

1 egg, lightly beaten

200g (7oz) brown sugar

1 cup plain flour

1 tsp baking soda

1 cup milk chocolate chips

1½ cups pecans, coarsely chopped

1 Preheat oven to 200°C (400°F). Line 2 cookie sheets with baking paper.

2 Combine peanut butter, butter, vanilla and egg in a bowl, then add the sugar, flour and baking soda. Mix thoroughly, then fold through chocolate and pecans.

3 Roll heaped tablespoonfuls into balls and place on the cookie sheets. Press lightly with the back of a fork and bake for 8–10 minutes. Cool on the cookie sheets.

Makes 30

Double Troubles

Preparation 15 mins **Cooking** 12 mins **Calories** 193 (each)

⅓ cup extra light olive oil

100g (4oz) milk chocolate, chopped

½ cup superfine sugar

1 tsp vanilla extract

1 egg, lightly beaten

1½ cups self-rising flour, sifted

½ cup hazelnut spread

50g (2oz) bittersweet chocolate chips

1 Line a baking tray with baking paper. Place oil and milk chocolate into a small saucepan over low heat. Cook, stirring with a metal spoon, for 2 minutes or until chocolate has melted. Remove to a bowl. Allow to cool for 5 minutes.

2 Add sugar, vanilla and egg. Mix well. Add flour and stir with a wooden spoon until just combined.

3 Roll mixture into balls, 2 teaspoonfuls at a time. Place onto the baking tray and flatten slightly.

4 Use the end of a wooden spoon to make an indentation in the center of each cookie. Fill each indentation with ½ teaspoon of hazelnut spread, then place bittersweet chocolate chips on top. Place tray in freezer for 15 minutes or until cookies are firm.

5 Preheat oven to 180°C (350°F). Bake cookies for 12 minutes or until firm to the touch. Cool for 5 minutes on the tray before transferring to a wire rack.

Makes 20

Florentines

Preparation 25 mins **Cooking** 10 mins **Calories** 276 (each)

125g (4¼ oz) butter, at room temperature

½ cup sugar

5 tbsps corn syrup

¼ cup plain flour

1 cup sliced almonds

½ cup candied cherries, chopped

½ cup walnuts, chopped

¼ cup mixed peel, chopped

150g (5oz) bittersweet chocolate

1 Preheat oven to 180°C (350°F). Line 4 oven trays with baking paper.

2 Cream butter and sugar, then beat in corn syrup. Sift in flour, add almonds, cherries, walnuts and peel and mix well.

3 Place tablespoonfuls of mixture onto a tray, leaving plenty of room for the cookies to spread. Using a knife, press each one out as flat and round as possible. Cook no more than 4 or 5 to a tray.

4 Bake for 10 minutes or until golden brown. Remove from oven and leave on tray for 5 minutes before transferring to a wire rack.

5 Meanwhile, melt chocolate in a bowl over simmering water. When the cookies are cold, ice with chocolate on their flat sides.

Makes 20

Fudge Chocolate Cookies

Preparation 20 mins **Cooking** 10 mins **Calories** 276 (each)

125g (4½oz) butter, chopped

1 tsp vanilla extract

1¼ cups brown sugar, firmly packed

1 egg

1 cup plain flour

¼ cup self-rising flour

1 tsp baking soda

⅓ cup cocoa powder

½ cup raisins

¾ cup macadamias, toasted and coarsely chopped

½ cup bittersweet chocolate chips

½ cup bittersweet chocolate melts, halved

1 Preheat oven to 180°C (350°F). Line 2 oven trays with baking paper.

2 Beat butter, vanilla, sugar and egg in a medium bowl with a blender until smooth.

3 Sift the flours together with the baking soda and cocoa powder, then stir into the butter mixture with the raisins, nuts and chocolate.

4 Drop rounded tablespoonfuls of mixture onto the trays about 4cm (1⅓in) apart, press each with a fork to flatten slightly. Bake for 10 minutes.

5 Stand the cookies for 5 minutes, then transfer to a wire rack to cool.

Makes 24

Hazelchocs

Preparation 20 mins **Cooking** 20 mins **Calories** 228 (each)

120g (4¼oz) butter
4 tbsps superfine sugar
4 tbsps brown sugar
1 cup plain flour
3 tbsps rice flour
2 tbsps cornstarch
2 tbsps instant coffee, plus 1 tsp
2 tbsps milk
3 tbsps hazelnuts, toasted and finely chopped
½ cup chocolate hazelnut spread
100g (4oz) bittersweet chocolate, melted

1 Preheat oven to 170°C (340°F). Lightly butter 2 baking trays.

2 Beat butter and sugars in a small bowl with a blender until pale and fluffy. Stir in sifted flours and 2 tbsps of the coffee in two batches, then stir in milk and nuts.

3 Roll tablespoonfuls into balls and flatten slightly. Place 3cm (1in) apart on the baking trays. Bake for about 20 minutes or until pale golden. Cool on a wire rack.

4 Meanwhile, combine hazelnut spread and chocolate in a bowl. Refrigerate, stirring often, until spreadable.

5 Join 2 cookies with 1–2 tsps of hazelnut chocolate. Repeat with remaining cookies.

Makes 16

Pecan Choc Biscotti

Preparation 15 mins **Cooking** 1 hr 20 mins plus 15 mins cooling **Calories** 4, 569 (per log)

280g (10oz) plain flour

85g (3oz) cocoa powder

1 tsp baking soda

1 tsp salt

1 cup superfine sugar

85g (3oz) sweetened butter

100g (4oz) pecans, ground, plus 50g (2oz) roughly chopped

150g (5oz) chocolate chips

3 eggs

2½ tbsps chocolate liqueur

1 Preheat oven to 170°C (340°F). Lightly butter a baking tray. Sieve flour, cocoa, baking soda and salt into a large bowl, add the sugar. Rub in the butter until the mixture resembles breadcrumbs. Stir through the ground pecans, chopped pecans and chocolate chips.

2 Beat the eggs with the chocolate liqueur and add to the other ingredients. Mix until a dough forms, and gently knead to bind all the ingredients.

3 Divide in half, and form each half into a log 4cm (1½in) high and 4cm (1½in) wide. Place on the baking tray, then bake for 30 minutes. Remove from oven and allow to cool for 15 mins. Turn oven down to 140°C (285°F). Using a serrated knife, cut logs into 1½cm (¾in) slices and return to baking tray. Bake for another 50 minutes until crisp.

Makes 25

Black Forest Gâteau

Preparation 30 mins **Cooking** 1 hr 10 mins **Calories** 1097

200g (7oz) bittersweet chocolate, chopped
3 cups self-rising flour
1 cup superfine sugar
¼ cup cocoa powder
1½ cups milk
3 eggs, lightly beaten
185g (6oz) butter, softened
2 tbsps cherry brandy
chocolate curls, to decorate

Cherry Cream Filling
2 cups heavy cream
⅓ cup superfine sugar
440g (1lb) canned pitted cherries, well drained

1 Preheat oven to 180°C (350°F). Place chocolate in a heatproof bowl set over a saucepan of simmering water and heat, stirring, until chocolate melts. Remove bowl from pan and set aside to cool slightly.

2 Sift together flour, sugar and cocoa powder into a bowl. Add milk, eggs and butter and beat for 5 minutes or until mixture is smooth. Beat in chocolate until mixture is well combined.

3 Pour mixture into a deep, buttered 23cm (9in) round cake tin and bake for 60 minutes or until cooked when tested with a skewer. Stand in tin for 5 minutes before turning onto a wire rack to cool.

4 To make filling, place cream and sugar in a bowl and beat until soft peaks form. Divide cream into two portions. Fold cherries into one portion.

5 To assemble cake, using a serrated knife, cut cake into three even layers. Sprinkle each layer with cherry brandy. Place one layer of cake on a serving plate, spread with half the cherry cream and top with a second layer of cake. Spread with remaining cherry cream and top with remaining layer of cake. Spread top and sides of cake with cream. Decorate top of cake with chocolate curls.

Serves 8

Cappucino Chocolate Cheesecake

Preparation 25 mins **Cooking** 35 mins **Calories** 860

1¼ cups chocolate wafers, crushed

⅛ tsp ground cinnamon

1 cup light cream cheese

1 cup sugar

1 cup cocoa powder

2 eggs

2½ cups sour cream

2 tbsp coffee liqueur

1 tsp vanilla extract

2 tbsps cocoa powder, for dusting

1 Preheat oven to 185°C (360°F). Stir together wafer crumbs and cinnamon. Pat into bottom of 22cm (8½in) springform pan.

2 Beat cream cheese until light and fluffy. Beat in sugar and cocoa powder, then beat in eggs. Stir in 2 cups sour cream, the coffee liqueur and vanilla. Turn into prepared pan and bake for 30 minutes or until set.

3 Spread remaining sour cream evenly over top. Return to oven for 1 minute. Cool to room temperature, then chill thoroughly, covered. Remove from springform pan. Just before serving, dust with extra cocoa powder.

Serves 8

Checkerboard Cake

Preparation 50 mins **Cooking** 35 mins **Calories** 889

2½ cups plain flour
1 tsp baking powder
¾ tsp baking soda
2 cups superfine sugar
250g (9oz) butter, softened
1½ cups buttermilk or milk
60g (2oz) white chocolate, melted
1 tbsp vegetable oil
60g (2oz) bittersweet chocolate, melted
white chocolate curls

Chocolate Filling

375g (13oz) milk chocolate, broken into pieces
280g (10oz) butter, chopped
1½ tbsps corn syrup

1 Preheat oven to 180°C (350°F). Sift together flour, baking powder and baking soda in a bowl. Add sugar, butter and buttermilk or milk and beat until smooth. Divide into 2 equal portions.

2 Combine white chocolate and half the oil and fold into one portion of mixture. Pour into a buttered and lined 18cm (6¾in) square cake tin. Combine bittersweet chocolate and remaining oil and fold into remaining portion of mixture. Pour into a second prepared 18 cm (6¾in) cake tin.

3 Bake for 30 minutes or until cooked when tested with a skewer. Stand for 5 minutes before turning onto wire racks to cool.

4 To make filling, place milk chocolate, butter and corn syrup in a heatproof bowl set over a saucepan of simmering water and heat, stirring, until smooth. Remove bowl from pan and chill for 30 minutes or until filling thickens and is easy to spread.

5 To assemble cake, cut each cake into six even strips. Place a strip of white cake on a rack, spread one side with a little filling and press a strip of chocolate cake against it. Repeat to make a base of alternating colors. Spread top with filling. Then use another four strips of cake to make a second layer so that colors alternate. Spread top with filling then use remaining strips of cake to make another layer. Spread remaining filling over top and sides of cake and decorate with chocolate curls.

Serves 12

Choc Meringue Cake

Preparation 40 mins **Cooking** 40–50 mins **Calories** 938

Hazelnut Meringue
160g (5½oz) ground hazelnuts
2 tbsps cornstarch
1¼ cups sugar
6 egg whites

Chocolate Filling
220g (8oz) sweetened butter
185g (6oz) bittersweet chocolate, melted
3 tbsps superfine sugar
2 cups whipping cream
2 tbsps brandy
125g (4½oz) ground hazelnuts

Chocolate Topping
160g (5½oz) bittersweet chocolate
2 tsps vegetable oil
½ cup whipped cream
8 strawberries, halved

Variation: You can use raspberries instead of strawberries in this recipe.

1 Preheat oven to 120°C (250°F). To make meringue, mix together ground hazelnuts, cornstarch and ¾ cup sugar. Beat egg whites until soft peaks form, add remaining sugar a little at a time and beat until thick and glossy. Fold into hazelnut mixture.

2 Mark three 20cm (8in) squares on baking paper and place paper on baking trays. Place meringue mixture in a pastry bag fitted with a small plain tip and pipe mixture to outline squares, then fill squares with piped lines of mixture. Bake for 40–50 minute or until crisp and dry.

3 To make filling, beat butter until soft. Add chocolate, superfine sugar and cream and beat until thick. Fold in brandy and hazelnuts.

4 To make topping, place chocolate and oil in the top of a double saucepan and heat over simmering water, stirring until chocolate melts and mixture is smooth. Remove top pan and set aside to cool.

5 To assemble cake, place a layer of meringue on a serving plate and spread with half the filling. Top with another meringue layer and most of the remaining filling. Cut remaining meringue into squares and position at angles on top of cake. Drizzle with last of the topping and decorate with cream and strawberries.

Serves 10

Chocafé Muffins

Preparation 12 mins **Cooking** 15 mins **Calories** 271

4 eggs
¾ cup superfine sugar
1 tsp vanilla extract
50g (2oz) butter, softened
½ cup plain flour
1 tsp baking powder
½ cup cocoa powder
2 tbsps instant coffee

Topping
6 x 4cm (1½in) chocolate mint squares
confectioner's sugar, for dusting
chocolate, finely grated

1 Preheat the oven to 190°C (380°F). Grease a 12-muffin pan. Beat eggs, sugar and vanilla extract together until thick and creamy. The mixture should hold a figure-of-eight shape when it reaches this stage.

2 Melt the butter. Sift flour, baking powder, cocoa powder and coffee into the egg mixture and fold in with butter.

3 Three-quarter-fill muffin cups with mixture. Bake for 12–15 minutes or until muffins spring back when lightly touched. Allow to cool for 5 minutes before turning onto a wire rack.

Topping

1 Cut a 1cm (⅓in) slit in the top of each muffin. Cut the chocolate mints in half diagonally and push the cut side into the slit in each muffin. Dust with confectioner's sugar and sprinkle with grated chocolate.

Makes 12

Chocky Muffins with Raspberry Sauce

Preparation 12 mins **Cooking** 12 mins **Calories** 432

250g (9oz) butter, softened
½ cup cocoa powder
100g (4oz) bittersweet chocolate, broken into pieces
1¼ cups sugar
4 eggs
2 tsps vanilla extract
1¼ cups plain flour
1 tsp baking powder

Mixed Berry Sauce
1 cup frozen mixed berries
½ cup raspberry preserve
½ cup pre-made chocolate sauce

1 Preheat oven to 180°C (350°F). Grease a 12-muffin pan. Place butter, cocoa powder and chocolate in a saucepan large enough to mix all the ingredients. Melt over a medium heat, stir in sugar and allow to cool.

2 Beat in eggs and vanilla. Sift over flour and baking powder and combine well. Three-quarter-fill muffin cups with mixture. and bake for 12 minutes.

Mixed Berry Sauce

1 Thaw berries and mash lightly. Place in a saucepan with preserve. Heat until preserve melts and berries are hot, then stir in chocolate sauce. Serve warm muffins with sauce immediately.

Makes 12

Chocolate and Orange Cheesecake

Preparation 30 mins **Cooking** 30 mins **Calories** 827

Base

60g (2oz) Graham Crackers, finely crushed

30g (1oz) butter, melted

¼ cup sugar

Filling

500g (18oz) cream cheese, softened

2 tbsps orange juice

finely grated zest of 1 large orange

¼ cup sugar

2 large eggs

½ cup chocolate chips

1 Preheat oven to 165°C.

Base

1 Combine crumbs, butter and sugar. Line four 10cm (4in) springform tins with baking paper, then press mixture evenly onto bottoms of tins.

2 Bake for 5 minutes.

Filling

1 Combine cream cheese, juice, zest and sugar in a blender, mix on medium speed until well combined. Add eggs one at a time. Stir through the chocolate. Divide filling evenly between tins.

3 Bake for 25 minutes. Cool before removing from tins.

Serves 4

Chocolate Babka

Preparation 30 mins **Cooking** 60 mins **Calories** 1110

250g plain flour
4 tbsps cocoa powder
1½ tsps baking powder
¾ tsp baking soda
½ tsp salt
250g (9oz) butter
250g (9oz) confectioner's sugar, sifted
1 tsp vanilla extract
4 eggs, separated
1 cup sour cream

Topping
1 cup chocolate chips
3 tbsps superfine sugar
4 tbsps raisins
½ cup chopped pecan nuts

1 Preheat oven to 180°C (350°F). Grease a 25cm (10in) tube cake pan. Sift together first 5 ingredients, then set aside. In a medium bowl, beat butter and sugar together in a blender until light and fluffy. Then beat in the vanilla extract.

2 Beat the eggs in one at a time. With mixer on slow speed, alternately beat the flour mixture and sour cream into the creamed mixture, beginning and ending with the flour mixture. Beat until just blended, do not over-beat.

3 Make the topping by taking a small bowl and combining all of the topping ingredients to make a crumb mixture.

4 Spread half of the cake mixture in the bottom of the prepared pan. Sprinkle with half of the crumb mixture. Pour in the remaining cake mixture and sprinkle with the remaining topping mixture. Press the crumb mixture in tightly so that it sticks to the cake.

5 Cut through the cake and crumbs in an up and down motion with a kitchen knife, then tap down to settle.

6 Bake in the preheated oven for 40 minutes, then cover the top of cake with aluminum foil and bake for a further 20 minutes. Leave the cake in the tin for about 30 minutes to allow to cool, then turn onto a cooling rack.

Note: Babka is a traditional sweet yeast-risen bread or cake.

Serves 6

Chocolate Banana Cake

Preparation 30 mins **Cooking** 1 hr **Calories** 665

125g (4¼ oz) butter
¾ cup sugar
2 eggs
2 over-ripe bananas
¼ cup yogurt
1¾ cups plain flour
¼ cup cocoa
2 tsps baking powder
1 tsp bicarbonate of soda
½ cup chocolate chips
chocolate curls

Chocolate Icing
1 cup confectioner's sugar
1 tbsp cocoa
1 tsp vanilla extract
1½ tbsps hot water

1 Chop butter roughly and place in the bowl of a blender. Add sugar. Process to combine. Add eggs, bananas and yogurt. Process to combine.

2 Sift in flour, cocoa, baking powder and baking soda and process briefly to just combine. Stir chocolate chips through cake mixture and pour into a 20cm (8in) square cake tin with a baking paper-lined base.

3 Bake at 180°C (350°F) for 50 minutes or until a skewer inserted in the middle comes out clean. Cool in tin for 10 minutes. Turn out onto a wire rack to cool. When cold frost with chocolate mixture and decorate with chocolate curls.

Chocolate Icing

1 Sift confectioner's sugar and cocoa into a bowl. Add vanilla extract and enough hot water to make a spreadable frosting.

Serves 6–8

Chocolate Caramel Cheesecake

Preparation 40 mins **Cooking** 40 mins **Calories** 632

Base

150g (5oz) Graham crackers,
finely crushed

50g (2oz) butter, melted

Filling

¼ cup evaporated milk

380g (13oz) canned caramel

1 cup pecan nuts, chopped

500g (18oz) cream cheese

½ cup sugar

2 eggs

1 tsp vanilla extract

¾ cup chocolate chips, melted

1 Preheat oven to 180°C (350°F).

Base

1 Combine crumbs and melted butter. Press mixture evenly into a 23cm (9in) springform tin. Bake for 8 minutes. Remove from oven and allow to cool.

Filling

1 Combine milk and caramel in a heavy-based saucepan. Cook over low heat until melted, stirring often. Pour over cookie base. Sprinkle pecans evenly over caramel layer and set aside.

2 Beat cream cheese at high speed with a blender until light and fluffy. Gradually add sugar, mixing well. Add eggs one at a time, whisking well after each addition. Stir in vanilla and melted chocolate, beat until blended. Pour over pecan layer.

3 Bake for 30 minutes. Remove from oven and run knife around edge of tin to release sides. Cool to room temperature. Cover and chill for 8 hours.

4 Decorate with a chopped flaky chocolate bar and chopped jersey caramels. Serve with whipped cream.

Makes 12 slices

Chocolate Espresso Cheesecake

Preparation 30 mins **Cooking** 40 mins **Calories** 802

Crust

1 cup chocolate cookie crumbs

2 tbsps melted butter

1 tbsp sugar

Filling

250g (9oz) bittersweet chocolate, chopped

1kg (2¼ lb) cream cheese

1 cup sugar

1 cup sour cream

2 large eggs

2 egg yolks

¼ cup espresso coffee

1 tsp vanilla extract

1 tbsp freshly ground coffee

Ganache

1 cup heavy cream

160g (5½ oz) bittersweet chocolate, chopped

1 tbsp instant espresso, dissolved in 2 tbsps water

1 Make the crust by mixing together all of the crust ingredients in a bowl. Press into the bottom of a 23cm (9in) springform tin. Ser aside and refrigerate until ready to use.

2 Make the filling by melting the chocolate in the top of a double boiler, then set aside to cool.

3 Cream the cream cheese and sugar until light and fluffy. Add the sour cream and mix, scraping down the sides of the bowl. Add eggs and egg yolks until well mixed. Then add the espresso, vanilla and ground coffee. Add chocolate and blend.

4 When well mixed pour mixture into prepared crust and place springform in a water bath. Bake at 180°C (350°F) for 45 minutes. When cooked turn off oven for about one hour before removing.

5 Make the ganache; bring cream to the boil on stove. Then pour over the chopped chocolate and let stand for about one minute. Stir to dissolve, then stir in the espresso.

6 Let cool at room temperature. Pour over top of cooled cheesecake, refrigerate to let set.

Serves 12

Chocolate Mascarpone Roulade

Preparation 30 mins **Cooking** 30 mins **Calories** 431

185g (6oz) bittersweet chocolate

¼ cup strong black coffee

5 eggs, separated

½ cup superfine sugar

2 tbsps self-rising flour, sifted

½ cup chocolate hazelnut spread

frosted rose petals, optional

Mascarpone Filling

375g (13oz) mascarpone

2 tbsps confectioner's sugar, sifted

2 tbsps brandy

1 Preheat oven to 160°C (325°F). Place chocolate and coffee in a heatproof bowl set over a saucepan of simmering water and heat, stirring, until smooth. Cool slightly.

2 Beat egg yolks until thick and pale. Gradually beat in superfine sugar. Fold chocolate mixture and flour into egg yolks.

3 Beat egg whites until stiff peaks form. Fold into chocolate mixture. Pour mixture into a buttered and lined 26 x 3cm. (10 x 1in) Swiss roll tin and bake for 20 minutes or until firm. Cool in tin.

4 To make filling, beat mascarpone, confectioner's sugar and brandy in a bowl.

5 Turn cakes onto a clean dish towel sprinkled with superfine sugar. Spread with chocolate hazelnut spread and half the filling and roll up. Spread with remaining filling and decorate with frosted rose petals.

Note: To make frosted rose petals, lightly beat egg white in a shallow bowl and dip in fresh, dry petals to lightly cover. Dip petals in superfine sugar, shake off excess and stand on baking paper to harden.

Serves 10

Coffee Muds

Preparation 30 mins **Cooking** 35 mins **Calories** 387

225g (8oz) Chocolate Graham Crackers

225g (8oz) butter, softened

225g (8oz) bittersweet chocolate

⅓ cup corn syrup

3 medium eggs, beaten

½ tsp vanilla extract

1 tbsp instant coffee

50g (2oz) white chocolate

1 Preheat the oven to 180°C (350°F). Line a 12-cupcake pan with cupcake papers. Place the crackers into a plastic bag, seal, then crush with a rolling pin. Melt 75g (2½oz) of the butter in a saucepan. Remove from the heat and mix in the crackers. Divide the mixture between the papers, pressing over the base and gently up the sides of each paper. Refrigerate for 20 minutes or until firm.

2 Put the remaining butter, chocolate and syrup into a double boiler. Heat gently, stirring, until melted. Remove from the heat and cool for 5 minutes. Beat in the eggs, vanilla extract and coffee.

3 Spoon the chocolate mixture over the bases and bake for 20 minutes or until just firm. Leave to cool for 5 minutes.

4 Meanwhile, melt the white chocolate in a double boiler. Drizzle over the cakes.

Note: These tasty treats are a hybrid of cupcake, brownie and muffin.

Makes 12

Five-Minute Chocolate Cake

Preparation 2 mins **Cooking** 3 mins **Calories** 1571

4 tbsps plain flour
4 tbsps sugar
2 tbsps cocoa
1 egg
3 tbsps milk
3 tbsps olive oil
3 tbsps chocolate chips
a small splash of vanilla extract

1   Add flour, sugar and cocoa to a microwave proof mug, and mix well. Add the egg and mix thoroughly. Pour in the milk and oil and mix well. Add the chocolate chips and vanilla, and mix again.

2   Put the mug in the microwave and cook for 3 minutes at full power. The cake will rise over the top of the mug, something like a souffle. Allow to cool a little, and tip out onto a plate if desired, or eat with a spoon directly from the mug.

Serves 1

Chocolate Spice Muffins

Preparation 10 mins **Cooking** 20 mins **Calories** 255

2¼ cups plain flour
¼ cup cocoa powder
3 tsps baking powder
1½ tsps ground cinnamon
¼ cup sugar
2 eggs
2 tsps vanilla extract
55g (2oz) butter, softened
1¼ cups milk
confectioner's sugar, for dusting

1   Preheat the oven to 200°C (400°F), and grease a 12-muffin pan. Sift flour, cocoa powder, baking powder and cinnamon into a bowl. Stir in sugar. Make a well in the center of the dry ingredients.

2   Lightly beat eggs and vanilla together and melt butter. Mix eggs, butter and milk together. Pour wet mixture into dry ingredients, and mix quickly until just combined.

3   Three-quarter-fill muffin cups with mixture. Bake for 15–20 minutes or until muffins spring back when lightly touched. Dust with confectioner's sugar to serve.

Makes 12

Blueberry Choc Chip Muffins

Preparation 15 mins **Cooking** 12 mins **Calories** 293

1 cup self-rising flour
½ cup superfine sugar
⅓ cup chocolate chips
1 egg, lightly beaten
¼ cup oil
¼ cup milk
100g (4oz) blueberries

Variation: You can use raspberries instead of blueberries.

1 Place flour, sugar and chocolate in a bowl and mix well. Mix together the egg, oil and milk, then stir into flour mixture. Add blueberries, stir until just combined.

2 Preheat oven to 200°C (400°F), or preheat an electric pie maker. Place a double layer of paper muffin cases in a muffin tin, or in an electric pie maker, if using. Divide the muffin mixture evenly between the cases.

3 If using the oven, bake for 10–12 minutes or until golden brown. If using an electric pie maker, close and cook for 5–6 minutes or until golden brown.

Makes 6

Index